Mending Clothes

An Upcycling Stitching Clothing Handbook for
Repairing Your Clothes Using Darning, Patching,
Sashiko, and Embroidery Techniques and Designs

By

Zera Meyer

Disclaimer

This publication is designed to provide competent and reliable information regarding the subject matter covered. However, the views expressed in this publication are those of the author alone, and should not be taken as expert instruction or professional advice. The reader is responsible for his or her own actions.

The author hereby disclaims any responsibility or liability whatsoever that is incurred from the use or application of the contents of this publication by the purchaser or reader. The purchaser or reader is hereby responsible for his or her own actions.

Table of Contents

Introduction

When last did you hemmed a pair of bad jeans, darned a sock, or patched a garment? Most of our forefathers were adept at repairing, mending, stitching, and reworking their clothes to extend their life span. It's all too simple to get anything trendy and cheap these days. Most of us have never been taught the abilities that our forefathers considered necessary. The ability to mend clothes can provide personal, environmental, financial, and systemic benefits. Even more, it's accessible - anybody can learn to mend to some extent.

Mending has existed for as long as there has been clothing. Ancient Egyptians would mend a garment 3 to 4 times before it is laid to rest inside someone's grave as embalming cloth, while Edo-era Japanese made use of "little stabs" of stitching to improve the resilience of their homespun fabrics. Throughout history, the underclass often did everything it took to increase the lifespan of their clothing since the fabrics themselves were "highly valuable, priceless, and worth preserving." Mending is not only a great way to prolong the life of garments and keep textile waste away from landfills but also a simple way to contribute to a sustainable fashion without needing to purchase anything new.

I believe people are recognizing that they can be their own sustainable heroes by mending what they have. They are beginning to understand that they don't need a large firm to be their sustainable hero, nor do they need to buy a garment produced from recycled plastic bottles to contribute to sustainability.

Mending can also be a meditative practice that "turns off" your mind to stress, anxiety, or boredom. And it's possible that as a result of this, we'll discover that "it is how we relate with our clothing that also needs to be mended."

Chapter 1

Clothe Mending Basics

What Is Mending?

Mending is the practice of fixing clothing with holes, tears, stains, or other evidence of wear to make it more useful and attractive. It's about making do with what you've got, accepting flaws, repairing what's broken, and resisting the notion that newer is better. Most mending entails hand sewing, which keeps your hands busy with repeated, comforting stitches. You can concentrate on the task at hand and use your imagination to create one-of-a-kind clothing. Consider an embroidered design on top of a coffee stain or a bright patch on top of a rip in your pants. It's a gradual, meditative process. It's both productive and satisfying. Plus, it's environmentally friendly.

Historical Evolution of Mending

Mending clothes is a very ancient practice. This means that mending was in vogue long before the Covid19 pandemic and shelter changed our daily lives.

The revival of the so-called "domestic" craftsmanship, rediscovered by feminists in the late 1990s and appreciated by visual artists since the early 2000s, coincided with a consumer shift known as fast fashion, with disastrous effects on humans and the environment. It became a global shopping frenzy that was to have an impact on the world. But now, as a result of the Covid 19 pandemic and subsequent quarantine (which has been relaxed drastically in recent times), retail sales of clothing in the U.S. have declined by more than 50%, and DIY products such as clothing repair have become a high-demand skill. With fast fashion in decline, is mending just the beginning?

Across history and cultures, people have mended cloth for practical and sentimental reasons to enhance their beauty, wearability, and utility. Enslaved Africans incorporated cloth and clothing discarded by their enslavers into their garments to show their social status. Japanese farmers have used "boro," a dense "rag-like" patchwork in making warmer and more durable clothing.

Also, Caribbean women who participated in the Dorcas Society, a charitable sewing circle formed during the cholera epidemic, made mending a part of their social

9

life. Born out of the philanthropy of the Victorian era, these societies came to exist throughout the world. The art of mending is no longer passed on as routinely as it once was, but thanks to countless books, YouTube videos, and online craft stores, most people can learn to attach buttons and mend hems.

But over the past two decades, our relationship with clothing has changed dramatically, especially in the United States. Whether or not we repair the clothes we buy is directly related to the value we place on them, and in the era of fast fashion, this is often not the case. Industrial and global supply chains, new technologies, and the proliferation of functional fabrics are also challenges for mending to become a widespread practice.

Between 2000 and 2015, global clothing manufacturing "doubled," greatly outpacing real need. On the other hand, Americans wear less than 20% of the clothes in their wardrobes and only "wear one garment 7-10 times and throw it away". In contrast, the new wave of fiber artists, along with "grassroots collectives like Fibershed," challenge the dysfunctional relationship between the fashion industry, an industry that accounts for "one-tenth of greenhouse gas emissions," and consumers' insatiable desire for products with scarce and perishable value and invites us to look at restoration in a new way.

The idea of upgrading and repairing clothes instead of throwing them away seems to be gaining more and more followers. Popular mediums like Martha Stewart, Spruce Craft, and the craft medium Interweave have brought the art and technique of mending into the mainstream. Some techniques are a bit more difficult, such as repairing tears and holes in knit and woven fabrics by mimicking the structure of the fabric. Several new books on visible repair techniques have appeared in the past year, expanding the subject and available resources.

Improvement can't solve everything that's wrong with the fashion industry, but it can make a difference. In a society that throws things away so quickly, making and repairing things by hand is a radical act. Repairing is a small way of thinking about what we consume, why we consume it, and what's important and valuable. It's essentially the spirit my mother instilled in me, not as a form of protest but as a way to take care of our precious clothes and manage our resources. In these times of unprecedented upheaval, we are challenged to reflect on our consumption and waste habits. In this context, my mending skills help connect the values of the past with a more sustainable future.

Why Is Mending Important?

There are many reasons, but here are my top five reasons why learning to mend your own clothes is important.

1. Mending reduces waste

This is important, especially in today's world of fast fashion. Most clothing today is made cheaply and quickly, which changes the mindset we associate with it. "Buy another t-shirt, it's only $5," we've stated how many times. But that's not a healthy way to think about clothing: one or two shirts may not seem like much, but they add up. Even if you say five times, "I'll buy another shirt, it'll only cost me $5"—that's five more shirts that end up in the landfill.

And while there are certainly times when a shirt (or anything else) can't be kept for repair, there are plenty of times when it can't. Most of the time it can be fixed, they just don't want to spend the time to fix it (or they don't care). And since the cost of repairing the shirt is higher than the price of the garment, the idea is to throw it away and buy a new one at a lower price; and a shiny new one at that. When you go from thinking, "Buy another shirt, it's only $5," to thinking, "Maybe I can fix this one," that's a big shift in consciousness. And it is very important if we want to reduce waste in our beautiful world.

2. It's free repairing your clothes

I think that says it all. If you know how to repair it yourself, it literally costs you nothing (except time). And while more difficult repairs and modifications should definitely be done by a professional, most repairs can be fixed (in my experience) with a needle and thread. Most people have a needle and thread at home. So, theoretically, you should be able to fix most of your everyday garments yourself and save money. It just takes time to figure out how to do it. But once you understand it, you'll be saving money in no time.

And actually, it not only saves you the trouble of taking your clothes to a mending shop to fix them. Remember the $5 shirt example from earlier? Here, too, you save money. Instead of buying a new one, you can literally keep the money in your pocket.

3. Things you love last longer

This is another self-evident truth. Everyone has a favorite piece that breaks or has a hole in it. Then comes despair. But not anymore. If you know how to repair clothes yourself, you can fix broken or holey pieces. This allows you to use your favorite piece for longer than expected. And most of the time, that means that when that favorite item is finally worn out a year or two later, it may not be available anymore (which is part of the intent of the fast fashion industry, and quite frustrating).

So if you can learn to repair them yourself, you'll be able to keep your favorite garments for longer.

4. Hone your hand-sewing skills

I have already mentioned that most of the repairs I do are hand-sewn. This is really true. Whether it's hemming, repairing a hole, or sewing a tear. My first choice for repairs is always hand sewing. It is easier to control and easier to handle in tight spaces. Because most of the time, the repairs are not that large.

I have rarely done repairs larger than a few centimeters. Besides, who would take out a sewing machine for a few centimeters? I doubt it.

14

5. Can become a side hustle

I can't even tell you how much money I've made just repairing people's clothes over the years. In all seriousness, it's actually a significant portion of my income.

People literally pay me to do the most basic and simple repairs, which are things they can do themselves in a few minutes or hours. But remember, repairs and modifications are two different things. Modifications are very complicated, and they cost more. And modifications require much more time and expertise than repairs and should be priced accordingly. But in most cases, they are not. But I guarantee you that if you can sew and repair your own clothes, people will come to you for advice when it comes to their own clothes.

Types Of Mending

The two most common types of mending are "visible mending" and "invisible mending".

Visible Mending: This method of repair involves highlighting the patched area by using colored threads, adding patches, or using some other visible mending techniques. Visible mending makes you feel like you are walking through an art gallery. There are many different ways to give a garment a new story through visible mending and most of these visible mending techniques will be covered in the subsequent chapters of this book.

Invisible Mending: This method of repair is used when the repaired area is not visible. It is better to go unnoticed. The aim is to bring the garment as close as possible to its original state. This is usually achieved by choosing a thread color that matches the garment, using small stitches, and hiding the stitches behind an existing hem or seam.

NB: We will focus mostly on visible mending throughout the pages of this book.

Chapter 2

Hand-Sewing Mending Stitches

Hand sewing is an old-fashioned chore that most people can outsource. You may have a good seamstress, but some clothing repairs and adjustments are much easier to do than you imagine. Whether you have popped buttons on your shirt, frayed pant hems, tears, ripped seams, or holes, the following hand-sewing stitches will help fix things with ease.

Let's touch on some basic sewing techniques to get you started before we discuss the hand-sewing stitches.

Basic Sewing Skills

Select The Right Needle and Thread

Choose yarns and threads closest to the makeup of the fabric piece you want to mend. Thickness is also vital; ensure working with a weight and thickness identical to your fabric. Your yarn or thread size will probably dictate the needle you will use. Note that the larger the eyelet of your needle is, the thicker the needle as well. So, if you're working with fabrics that are delicate in nature, you might want to go with a smaller eyelet needle to avoid creating undesired hole spots in your fabric.

Thread The Needle

There are several methods for threading a needle, but with consistent practice, it becomes simpler. To ease the process, you can lick the thread's tip or have the end folded to insert. Choose the method you are okay with and don't overthink it.

Starting and Ending Your Stitching

You can begin sewing by tying a knot at your thread's end; this works well for thin thread. Nevertheless, a knot would be so obvious if the threads are thick; in such instance, multiple stitches over each other should be sewn, setting aside an underside tail with which your stitches will thread on much later. This is how you'll also end your project.

Hand-Sewing Stitches

Running Stitch

The running stitch is the most basic of all hand-sewing stitches and forms the basis for all other forms of sewing. Running stitches may seem simple, but they can still be incredibly effective for repairing clothing.

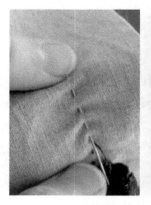 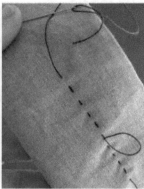

Below are the common applications of running stitches.

- For sewing patches on garments (such as a knee patch).
- For mending hem at the ending of pant legs or jacket sleeves.
- For reattaching straps or other pieces of fabric to the main piece.

After sewing, the running stitch will look the same on the two sides of the joined fabric.

Instructions for sewing a running stitch

To sew a running stitch, the needle and thread must be threaded between the overlapping fabrics without giving a backstitch. A straight stitch is sewn. These can be close or far apart. The following are the steps for sewing running stitches.

1. Thread the needle and knot the thread.
2. Attach the knot to the inside of the fabric at the point where the running stitch is to be sewn.
3. If sewing over several layers of fabric, then align the edges.
4. If necessary, secure with pins.
5. Pass the needle through the fabric from the bottom up, weaving the needle into the fabric.
6. Repeat the process until the desired area is sewn.
7. Secure the thread inside the seam or seam allowance and cut the thread.

Backstitch

Backstitch is a higher form of the running stitch, in which the stitch is made with one step backward and two steps forward along the line of your stitching. With backstitch, one side looks like a simple running stitch, but the other side is a series of overlapping stitches.

Backstitch is a very strong and flexible technique, suitable for mending badly damaged areas. Backstitch is used for the following applications.

- Reattaching zippers that have come loose.
- Ripped pockets
- Repairing torn or frayed seams on pants, shirts, and jackets.

In cases where running stitches can be used, backstitch can also be used. It is stronger and lasts longer but takes longer to sew.

Instructions for sewing a backstitch

1. Begin by sewing a small stitch.
2. Insert the needle back into the stitch's end where the thread was pulled out

3. Another stitch should be made and repeat the process above. These stitches should appear as though they are overlapping.

Whip Stitch

The whip stitch is a little more complex compared to the simple running stitch, consisting of short diagonal stitches.

The whip stitch can fix:

- Ripped seams on pants, shirts, and jackets
- Split open pockets
- Split open hems at the bottom (not at the actual hem stitch)

The thread's color used should be the same as the fabric you'll be sewing into since there would be some thread visibility after it is sewn.

Instructions for sewing a whip stitch

1. Thread the needle and pull it via the top fabric, ensuring the knot is between the two pieces of fabric.
2. Sew through the bottom fabric, exiting in the same spot where you began with the top fabric. This will secure your starting stitches
3. Needle through the bottom fabric to create a diagonal stitch along the fabric's edges. The needle and thread have to exit the fabric's top to secure it in place.
4. The above process should be repeated until you arrive at your fabric's ends. Remember to secure the stitches.

Buttonhole Stitch (Blanket Stitch)

As the name suggests, this stitch is used to finish the blanket's edges or create buttonholes.

Instructions for sewing a buttonhole stitch

1. Push and pull the needle all the way via the fabric, starting from the back.
2. Again, push and pull in the needle via the back of the fabric. By so doing, a loop has been created.
3. Pull the needle via the loop.

4. Steps 1-3 should be repeated, spacing your stitches approximately 1cm apart if working on a blanket.

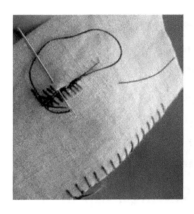

Slip Stitch (Ladder Stitch)

Slip stitching can be used to close a seam or hole, as is the case with the whip stitch, but the stitch itself will be invisible.

Sadly, mastering this stitching technique is somewhat challenging at first. This type of stitch is better suited for mending holes in more prominent areas where the whip stitch thread would be too visible. The slip stitch is also widely employed to make seams hidden in between a flat edge's double fold edges. Because you create ladders with your threads when making this stitch, it's also known as a ladder stitch.

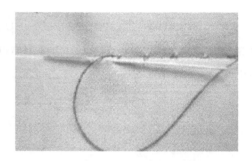

Slip stitch is not as strong as whip stitch and should only be used to mend small holes or tears. The slip stitch can make garment problems literally disappear with patience and the right skill.

Instructions for sewing a slip stitch

1. Your fabric should be folded to the wrong sides of both sections.

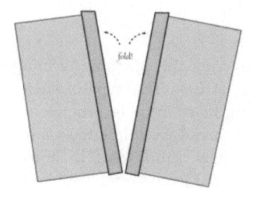

2. Insert the threaded needle under the fold to conceal the knot.

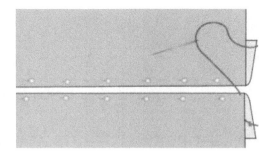

3. Pull out the threaded needle from the folded edge.
4. Take out some fabric beneath the opposite side of the fold.

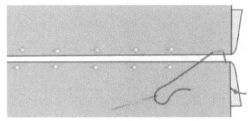

5. Pull out the needle and re-insert it at the opposite side

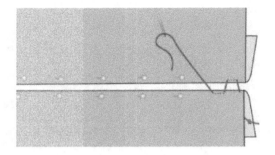

6. Repeat the process until the opening is closed. Don't forget to tie your knot at the end; same for every other stitch covered previously.

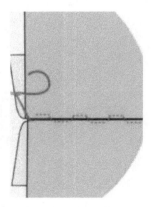

Overcast Stitch

This stitch is used to finish an edge that can be sewn either by hand or machine. An overcast stitch gives your edges a neat look and prevents the raw edges of fabrics from unraveling. The overcast stitch can also be used in mending a tear.

Instructions for sewing an overcast stitch

1. Thread your needle with a single thread and securely knot the ends of the two threads.
2. As shown in the image below, push the needle to the top of the fabric.

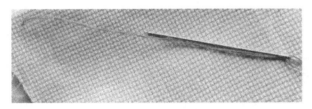

3. Bring the needle to the back, a thread distant from where you originally came up.

4. The thread should be looped while separating the two threads via the needle at the back. Push the needle up. This will be your first overcast stitch.

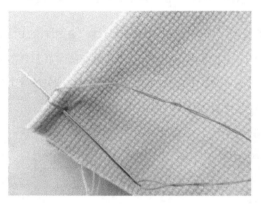

5. You'll have to go through the entire process again. Come up from behind, a little apart from your first stitch.

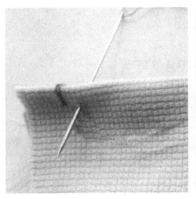 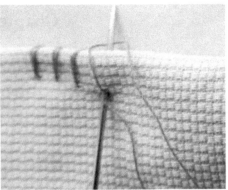

6. Repeat in this manner until the entire edge has been completed. The stitch on the back of the fabric is seen in the image below.

Chapter 3

Clothe Mending Tips

Here are some cloth mending tips to get acquainted with as you prepare to repair your clothes.

1. Keep the fabric taut and free of folds to avoid puckering. Using embroidered hoop is a good way to hold down a large section of a fabric that's sturdy, but if you're unable to get hold of one, you can use an adhesive freezer paper or a tear-away, heat-away, or wash-away stabilizer.

2. A minor rip in a new cloth can withstand any unwanted expansion once repaired. However, if worn out, the area is likely to wear again.

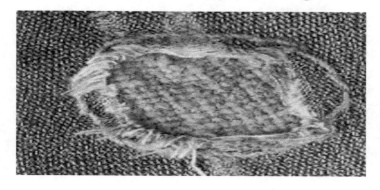

It's also possible that the encircling fabric isn't sturdy enough to sustain the repair. In this case, ensure your new stitches are much further from the hole or weak area to give them something to grip onto.

3. Long floats or patch areas not secured might catch and rip, resulting in a worse repair than before. Ensure any excess fabric of the patched area is stitched down or trimmed well enough.

4. Ensure you don't use long thread lengths when darning an area. This is because pulling long threads back and forth when darning can distort the shape of the darned piece

5. Repair as quickly as feasible, even if it's only a quick remedy

6. Iron the fabric first, if possible, to have it aligned

7. Washing a fabric before mending is not recommended because it can worsen the damaged area.

8. Always work in well-lit areas

9. After you've decided on your materials, you'll need to figure out how to fix the hole or worn-out region. There are several approaches to darning your hole that will produce varied results. Darning from the front gives you greater control over the shape of the darn and allows you to see more of your yarn and pattern on your knitwear's front. Darning from behind will result in a more natural-looking repair that mimics the shape of the hole.

 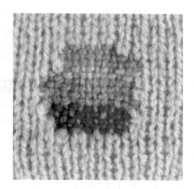

A darn from the front   A darn from the back

If you have thin knitwear that needs only reinforcement, swiss darning is the technique to apply. It will retain the knitwear's elasticity and appear to be a knitted fabric. You can also use swiss darning to fix holes, but I would only advise this for thick knits, except you have excellent eyesight and a lot of patience.

10. I believe that getting your tension just perfect is the secret to a great mend. It's important not to pull too tightly or too loosely. It's just a matter of getting used to it with practice.

11. This may seem self-evident, but visible repair ought to be seen, so choose colors you adore, a technique you enjoy, and create designs you relish. It can truly be whatever you need it to be! You must be comfortable wearing it, whether it is vibrant and bright or modest and plain. Use your creativity.

A Short message from the Author:

Hey, I hope you are enjoying the book? I would love to hear your thoughts!

Many readers do not know how hard reviews are to come by and how much they help an author.

I would be incredibly grateful if you could take just 60 seconds to write a short review on Amazon, even if it is a few sentences!

>> Click here to leave a quick review

Thanks for the time taken to share your thoughts!

Chapter 4

Clothe Mending Techniques and Design

Darning

Darning is a stitching technique that resembles a woven patch used to mend holes or damaged areas in a knitted fabric, such as socks and sweaters, but it can also work well for woven fabrics, such as denim. Darning is usually done by hand; however, it can also be done with a sewing machine. Hand darning uses the darning stitch, which is made up of the running stitch where the thread is woven in rows along the fabric's grain, with the direction of the stitching reversed at each row's end and then having the resulting framework being filled in, as though being weaved.

Weft and warp yarns make up a fabric. The weft is a vertically running yarn, while the warp is a horizontally running yarn. They form the fabric by interlocking with one another. The darning stitch is used in rebuilding the weft and warp of a fabric's damaged section.

Darning Techniques

There are several darning techniques you can use that suit a variety of mending projects, whether darning socks or learning how to repair a hole in a sweater, each with its own unique look. Let's take a look at some of them below.

Weave Darning

Weave darn is the basic all-purpose darn used by most people. It is what they think of when they think of darning. Although it is not invisible, this darning technique works for several kinds of holes.

To avoid a too-airy finished weave, use a darning thread that's a bit thicker than the actual knit material. You can also make a tighter weave when you close up the space of your threads or using double threads in a single direction.

Making a Weave Darning Stitch

1. Starting from either the right or left side, stitch some rows down the hole and to one side. Work horizontally, weaving the needle across and beneath the stitches in that row.

2. Work horizontally, back and forth; weave across and beneath the stitches, and alternate on each row, i.e., across-beneath-across on the first row, then beneath-across-beneath on the next row, and so on. On getting to where the hole is, ensure the thread is slowly pulled through while continuing as you previously did on the other side.

3. As soon as the patch you've made is a little bigger than the size of the hole, turn it over, working vertically top-down. Ensure the horizontally patched work is kept inside by starting somewhat close to the hole so the edges do not get bulky.

4. Weave across and beneath the horizontal threads. When you have covered the hole, complete the process with the ends behind.

It's noteworthy that the weave darning technique changes the fabric's appearance. The knit's initial looping structure is substituted with a sturdy weave. The darned region loses its stretch as a result of this. This might not be an issue in any way. However, you can partially make up for this when you work in a diagonal form in step 3 rather than vertically. Conversely, work the entire darn diagonally for a more elastic finish. Unfortunately, doing so would make you lose the uniform spacing of the initial stitches as your guideline, making an even and clean finish more difficult.

Swiss Darning or Duplicate Stitch

You can use swiss darn (duplicate stitch) in knits in reinforcing weakening sections before a hole appears by simply using a darning or tapestry needle to work over the knit's main stitches. This preserves the knit fabric's existing form and elasticity, and if you use identical thread, it can be nearly unnoticeable. Using a thread that's identical to or slightly thinner than the main knit will ensure the covered region isn't excessively heavy and bulky compared to other regions of the garment.

If you want to use a contrasting color and you prefer to totally cover the main stitches, select a thread that's slightly thicker than the main knit.

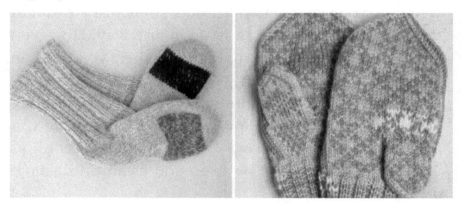

Making a Swiss Darning Stitch

1. Start from behind and pass the needle via a stitch's center while following the stitch's loop above and beneath the two threads of the top stitch

2. Pass the needle back via the center of your first stitch and above via the center of the next stitch to it. Proceed down the row. Making a mental note of each stitch in the shape of a "V" could help make your stitching a little easier.

3. To go a row up, the needle should be pushed via the center of the stitch you worked last and up via the center of the stitch just above, i.e., beneath a horizontal bar. Proceed down this row and work in the reverse direction.

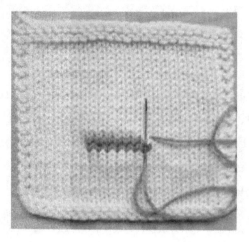

4. Go over the area to be reinforced again and again. Complete with the ends behind.

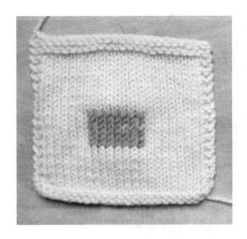

Pattern Darning

What if you could mend holes in cloth while also embroidering — a practical and decorative stitch in one? This is the whole point of pattern darning. It's essentially darning in a pattern using consistent, uniform stitches stitched according to a design you've planned ahead of time. The basic stitch employed here is the running stitch, formed in a set pattern, vertically or horizontally.

Although pattern darning has been around for generations, it is not as well-known as other embroidered stitches. The potential of this stitch, on the other hand, is limitless. Nothing beats it as a border design.

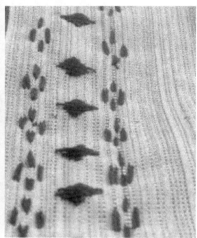

Fabrics For Making Pattern Darning

This stitching technique works best on evenweave (uniform fibers) fabrics such as linen, in which the weave (warp and weft threads) can be seen. The threads must be counted to determine the number of threads to be filled and left alone.

Pattern darning can be done with embroidery floss. It all depends on the fabric you're using for pattern darning. Sock wool is obviously the logical choice for pattern darning when fixing a hole in a sock. For the pattern to be apparent, a contrast or complementing color is usually used.

How To Do Pattern Darning

This stitch is typically used as a border or filler stitch by working small running stitches across the fabric's warp or weft thread. They are sometimes worked diagonally, though this is pretty uncommon.

Because this is a counted thread embroidery technique, the number of threads every stitch covers is always checked to ensure the pattern is consistent.

When you make the darning stitches through the warp and the weft threads together, it is then known as damask darn.

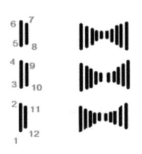  

Darning Tools

Darning requires the use of a tapestry needle, scissors, and thread in your preferred color. The needle and thread size you use will be determined by the project to be mended (we talked about this at the beginning of chapter 3). Other tools used are:

- Darning Egg

A darning egg is used to ensure you maintain the curvature of the fabric being mended, especially when darning socks, thereby preventing crooked, deformed socks. Darning eggs are named after their rounded egg form and are typically built from sturdy materials like wood or stone.

 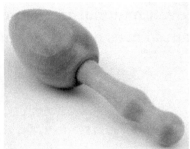

- Darning Mushrooms

Darning mushrooms feature a round top that is ideal for keeping the structure of your garment while darning. This tool is very useful because it has a flat bottom that may lay on a smooth surface to keep you balanced.

Patching

Patching is a method of securing a fabric patch across or underneath a hole. It may be done using either a knitted or woven material, but it works better with woven material and larger holes, such as those in your pant's knees or in your shirt's open elbows.

You can make your own patches or purchase them from a store.

The patches you make yourself from scrap fabrics should closely resemble the fabric you want to mend. You can sew the fabric above the hole, underneath the hole, or on both sides of the hole.

Extra tip: If you're making your own patches, you may need to secure the edges to keep them from fraying.

Patches gotten from the store are usually sewn or ironed onto the mended area. Iron-on patches use fabric glue that melts on the mended area when heated.

Sew-on patches take a bit more time to apply, but they may stick on better than iron-on patches (if you intend washing and drying the garment often).

PatchingTechniques

You can use different patching techniques for mending; we briefly touched on some of them earlier, but let's go into more detail below.

Iron-On Patch

These can be embroidered and non-embroidered patches that you can stick on the area to be mended using heat. This is the simplest method for appending patches. The sticky side of these patches is triggered when you apply heat. Some come with a removable covering layer, while others have a plasticky backside.

Attaching an Iron-On Patch

1. Grab the patch, which you can decide to either cut into fun shapes or leave as is.

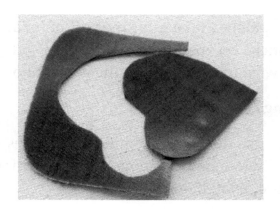

2. Set the iron-on patch in place (if it's a hole, cover it with the patch completely with ¼" all around it). Set the iron to a cotton temperature
3. Sprinkle some water behind the patch and place a sheet of ironing cloth (any thin cotton material) above it. This is to prevent the patch from being damaged by the heat.
4. Iron uniformly with the heated iron for about 20-30 seconds

Extra tip: To reinforce your patch, you can sew a running stitch along the patch's edges with a thread that matches the patch.

Note: Make sure your iron's heat setting is for a cotton material. Patches on elastic materials, leather, waterproof rainwear, and nylon fabrics should not be ironed since the heat may damage the material.

Applique Patch

This patch can be appliqued to the garment's front either by hand or machine. Hand applique (whose edges are turned under) uses a hand sewed blanket stitch, while machine applique uses tightly bunched zig zag stitches around the patch's edges.

Reverse Applique Patch

Reverse applique is exactly what it sounds like: applique done backward. In reverse applique, the patch is placed behind the fabric hole and sewn in place all around the hole's edges, and then the topmost fabric is ripped to reveal the applique patch beneath it, as opposed to applique, where the applique patch is placed on the front of the fabric hole.

Reverse Applique Fabrics to Use

Any fabric suitable with the color of the primary fabric can serve as the applique patch. Opposing textures, colors, etc., are preferable. Velvet, sequin fabric, and other textured materials, as well as lace and other sheer materials, are among my preferences. When the appliqué patch is sheer or visible, such as lace or eyelet material, it can create an attractive peekaboo effect.

Aside from the attractive usage of reverse applique to decorate fabric, one practical application is to patch holes in clothing.

Stitching a Reverse Applique Patch

1. To make this applique, trace the design onto the primary fabric. Also, draw a second line, 1/4-inch on the inside.

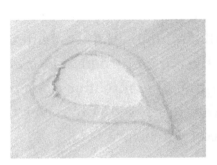 

2. Cut at 1/2 inch or less along the second line to the design line (under is excellent). Cut no further than the design line. Pin the applique fabric around the design to hold it in place.

3. Gently turn underneath the edges with a needle, press in place with your fingers, and hand stitch to secure it to create the design.

4. Whip stitches can be made around the edge. I prefer making a small running stitch beneath the folded edges to join the edges turned under and the fabric beneath so that the stitching does not appear outside. Another approach is to cover the folded area with blanket stitches.

Overhand Handmade Patch

This patch is stitched from the garment's face, i.e., the right side. If a thick fabric is being patched, use a thin thread to create the overhand patch; otherwise, it will protrude.

Stitching an Overhand Patch

1. Make a square shape in the existing hole. Cut a square of fabric that is a little larger (about ½") than the size of the hole. ¼" of the edges should be pressed inside.
2. Maintain its position over the hole and stitch down the edge with a basting stitch.
3. Flip the garment over so the wrong side is facing out. The hole's edge and the patch fabric will be in line. Stitch an overcast stitch all the way around the edge.

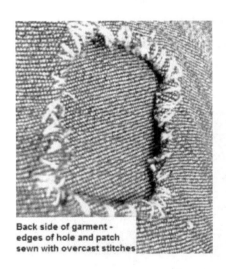

Back side of garment - edges of hole and patch sewn with overcast stitches

Sashiko

In pre-industrial Japan, fabric was in short supply, and so patches, scraps, and simple stitches were used to mend garments to make them last longer.

This is sashiko, and this method of mending wasn't ever intended to be invisible. Instead, it's intended to draw attention to rips, tears, frays, and fringes on a specific garment using contrasting thread stitches. Sashiko literally translates to "little stabs," which aptly uses the famous simple running stitch that characterizes this mending style. In sashiko, what governs the repair is the contours of the damage, which makes the garment's reinvention into something superior to what it used to be, i.e., a sturdier fabric and a much more beautiful design.

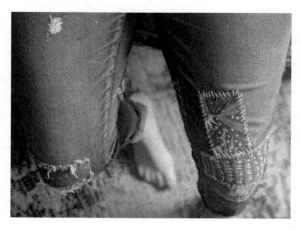

Sashiko uses the running stitch, created when the needle is inserted via the fabric while loading multiple stitches onto the needle simultaneously before you pull it through. This makes the most of your needle's length and produces a line of uniformly spaced stitches. On the other hand, the running stitch can also be used in stitching a circle, square, triangle, and any other shape's outline.

Keep in mind that garments are made up of fibers, which typically wear and tear with time. So, ensure you think about the grain and weight of the fabric you want to mend. Denim, for example, is slow to tear, so keep your threads approximately ½" from the patch's edge to prevent the edges from fraying through the mending stitches.

It's totally acceptable if the stitches are not perfect. Each piece mended bears the maker's signature, and the rustic quality simply adds to its beauty.

Slowing down, being intentional, and remembering the inventiveness that can be achieved when using a simple needle and thread is what sashiko requires us to do.

Tools and Materials

Only a few basic items are required for sashiko mending. They'll make your mending even more effortless once you've included them in your sewing toolkit. If you're a newbie to mending with sashiko, practicing with a template or pattern is a fantastic idea.

Sashiko Needle

Sashiko needles are long, robust, and designed specifically for running stitches, meaning it's built to be loaded with several stitches before being pulled through the fabric.

They are available in a variety of sizes; traditional ones are around 2 inches long, whilst modern ones are shorter and feature a wider eye for quicker threading.

Sewing Thread

Sashiko thread, which is normally recommended for the best results, is constructed of durable, heavy-weight cotton. It's available in a number of colors, though white is still the most preferred since it looks great with an indigo fabric.

You can use embroidery floss as an alternative; the difference is in the glossy texture and the loose threads, which can be pulled out for thinner stitches; as a result, the stitching will have a somewhat different look and feel. Pearl cotton in sizes 8 or 12 is the most popular embroidery floss alternative.

Cotton Fabric

Sashiko looks the nicest on a mix of loose-weave linen or cotton. Since sashiko thread is thick, it will reveal puckering very readily if the fabric is woven too tightly. The origin of Sashiko mending is cotton fabric, but it may also be done on denim. Because it's thick, resilient, and practical, denim is an excellent choice for visible mending. The patch of the fabric should be matched to the fabric of the garment you want to mend, just like you would with thread. The goal is to make the garment stand out.

Sashiko Thimble

A thimble is the best way to protect your finger. You wear a sashiko thimble at the bottom of your dominant hand's middle finger, similar to a ring. To use it for sewing, thread the needle and drive it through the fabric with the eye-end against the protecting pad of the thimble.

They are available in several sizes, so make sure you get the right one for your finger. Metal thimbles are the most durable option. On the other hand, leather is more flexible and enables the skin of your finger to breathe for long durations while working.

Additional Tools

Support your sashiko sewing kits with;

- Scissors for cutting patches, clipping thread, and snipping fabric
- Straight or safety pins for holding the patches in place
- Transfer (tracing) paper for transferring the pattern onto the fabric

- Tailor's chalk or vanishing fabric marker for sketching grid lines for stitches or highlighting the borders of a patch
- Ruler for measuring and making straight lines
- Pattern of any design to highlight the areas you will stitch. Sashiko stitching would look beautiful with any pattern. The all-time preference are Japanese geometric patterns, but you can as well draw inspiration from several stitching and embroidery cultures. Starting with the fundamentals is always a good choice, such as the geometric patterns. Some samples are given below;

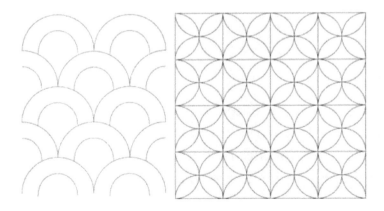

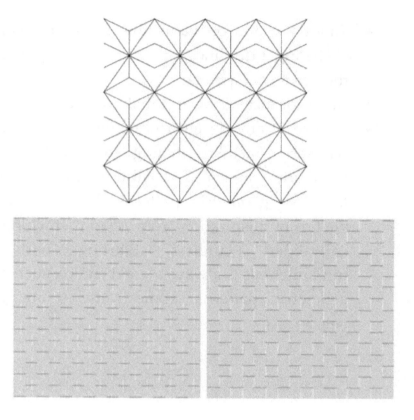

Embroidery

Embroidery is a technique for decorating knitted or woven fabric using thread. It's a terrific way to dress up a piece of clothing or personalize an object, disguise or highlight any stitches used to patch holes and hide stains.

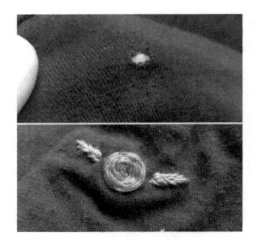

a stitched hole using an embroidered rose

Note: Detailed video instructions or gifs with sample patterns on making simple embroidered designs, such as hearts, flowers, stars, leaves, etc., can be found on Youtube, Pinterest, and over the internet as a whole.

Embroidery is normally done using embroidery floss, but you might also use yarn, ribbons, or plain old sewing thread, based on the fabric material you are working on. Don't be reluctant to try new things!

You can easily do embroidery on fabrics that are taut than limp. And this is the reason several people use embroidery hoops to keep their fabric taut and secure when stitching, allowing for uniform stitching and preventing puckering.

A hoop will make your stitching very easy, even though it isn't entirely necessary.

It will also be helpful if you use the right needle. If you are sewing with embroidery floss, a crewel needle (also known as embroidery needle) should be used, a chenille needle if you are sewing with ribbon or yarn, or a tapestry needle if you are sewing cross-stitch embroidery on open-weave materials.

The possibilities are limitless once you have mastered a few fundamental stitches like running stitch and backstitch.

The end... almost!

Hey! We've made it to the final chapter of this book, and I hope you've enjoyed it so far.

If you have not done so yet, I would be incredibly thankful if you could take just a minute to leave a quick review on Amazon

Reviews are not easy to come by, and as an independent author with a little marketing budget, I rely on you, my readers, to leave a short review on Amazon.

Even if it is just a sentence or two!

So if you really enjoyed this book, please...

>> Click here to leave a brief review on Amazon.

I truly appreciate your effort to leave your review, as it truly makes a huge difference.

Chapter 5

Clothe Mending Projects

In this chapter, we will apply a number of the mending techniques already discussed in repairing different fabrics.

Jeans

Hand Sewing Straight Tear

1. Trim away the frayed edges. You will have to remove the surplus threads or frayed ends created by the tear before you can even mend your jeans properly. Grab a pair of scissors and aim to cut as close as possible; you would want to remove any protrusions, but you also do not want to ruin any material that could be saved.

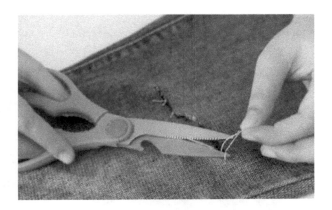

2. Sew the tear. Smaller tears can generally be repaired without the use of patches if you've not lost significant material. Your jeans should be turned inside out first; when you do, the new seams will be less noticeable when you sew. Sew an overcast stitch back and forth with a sewing needle and thread till the rip is repaired. Ensure the stitches are close together as possible.

Use a thread that matches the rest of the jeans' seams. This will most likely be a black or white thread. If the rip is visible and distant from natural seams, it is preferable to go for a color that complements the rest of your jean's typical color (mostly blue or black)

74

3. Cut off any surplus thread and material that protrudes. Cut any leftover protruding material and surplus thread. After you've sewed up the rip, you can trim off the excess fabric. Ensure the sewing thread is cut closer to the material of the jean.

4. Iron to press down the mended area. After the repair, iron to press down the rip you've just sewn to seal it up and smoothen out any creases.

Patching a Hole

There are different methods of patching a hole on a Jean. They are:

Method 1 – Using Iron-On Patch

In chapter 4, under the *"Patching Techniques: Iron-On Patch"* section, we provided detailed steps with illustrations on how to patch holes in your jeans using the iron-on patch method. So, kindly refer to the above-named section.

Method 2 – Using Embroidery Stitches

1. Trim the rough edges of the torn area and then use chalk or vanishing ink pen to draw a border around the hole.

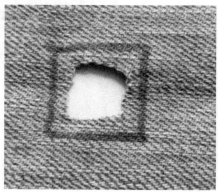

2. Begin sewing, using a thick embroidery thread to stitch in the order shown in the diagram below, from A-H (top-down).

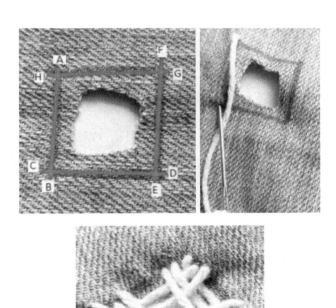

Sew over the hole I-P (left-right) with the same stitches used before in the sequence below.

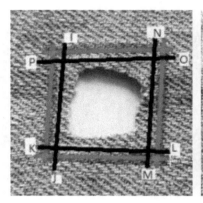 

Continue stitching until the hole is completely filled.

There is no caste-in-stone method for patching up holes in jeans using embroidery. As earlier mentioned, you can sew embroidery designs over holes using flowers, roses, or any shape you can imagine. Be creative!

Method 3 – Sashiko Stitching

1. Make sure you use a patch that's bigger than the hole. A bigger patch will ensure you don't have to patch the same area in the near future.

2. Flip your jeans inside out and lay the patch on top of the hole, securing it using safety pins.

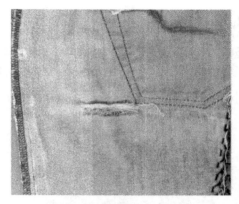

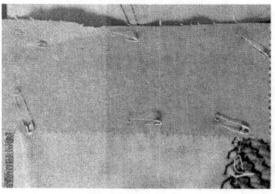

3. Draw a 1/4 inch grid over the spot you want to stitch with a ruler and a vanishing fabric marker (the whole section of the patch, in my case).

   N.B: The sashiko stitching starts from here onwards and there is no limit to what pattern and method you can apply. I have just applied a simple approach below, but you can decide to use any of the sashiko geometric pattern samples I shared in chapter 4 under the *Additional Tools* section of the *Sashiko* technique and use a transfer (tracing) paper and a vanishing fabric marker to transfer the pattern onto where your patch will be stitched.

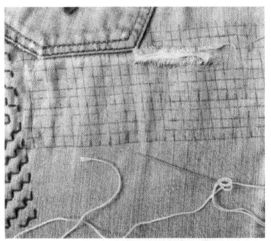

4. Sew a ¼" running stitch along the patch's length with the grid to guide you. Reverse the stitch when you begin a new row, such that every second row is still the same.

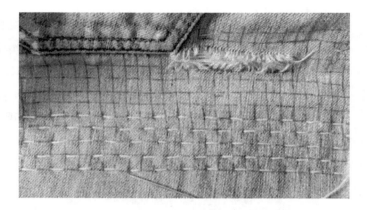

5. You might need to pause at this point because the hole has been patched and the jeans have been strengthened in this whole area.

Take off the safety pins and you can decide to leave the vanishing fabric marker until when next you wash the jean for it to vanish, or you can use a heat-sensitive pen and a pressing iron like I chose to do here to remove the marker.

6. With a fabric that's lighter, the cut edges beneath should be ironed, Pinning the patch to secure it.

7. Sew the patch with a whip stitch.

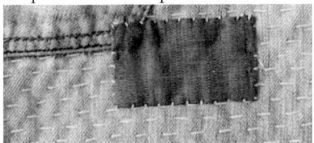

8. Draw a ¼" grid on the patch with your fabric marker.

9. Stitch in alternating horizontal rows across the intersection of the lines with a running stitch of smaller length.

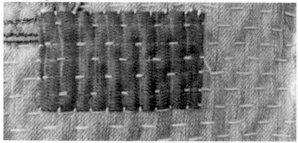

10. Vertically repeat this procedure. Crosses will form as a result of your stitches. The mended jeans using the sashiko technique is now complete, beautiful isn't it.

Remember, your creativity can give you better results.

Method 4 – Inside Patch

1. Make sure you use a patch that's bigger than the hole

2. Completely cover the hole by placing the patch inside the garment and pin it in place.

3. Thread a needle and tie a knot
4. Sew a whip stitch from the inside to join the patch and garment, parallel to the seam. The raw edges should be folded inwards and sewn for a neater finish

5. Tie and trim the thread off.

6. Flip the garment wrong side out and trim the patch to fit, leaving adequate room for the patch to fray without pulling free.

Denim Button Hole Repair

1. Thread your needle and start sewing a buttonhole stitch a little beyond where the buttonhole started to separate. You'll be working from right to left in this case.

2. The needle should be pulled midway through, looping the thread and loop over the needle.

3. Thread the needle across the loop, pulling the thread firmly to create the knot.

4. Repeat this process until the button hole's damaged area is fully stitched.

5. Tie and trim the thread off.

Denim Hem Repair

1. Make sure you use a patch that's bigger than the hole

2. All except one of the patch's edges should be pressed inwards, and this piece should be folded in half.

3. Set the patch's raw edge in an upturned manner, perpendicular to the damaged area and inside. This should be pinned in place.

4. Along the raw edge's damaged area, sew a running stitch and tie off to finish. This stitch

should be sewn just before where the damaged area started.

5. Fold over the patch and ensure it covers the damaged area, including the stitches you just did.
6. Sew a whip stitch around the patch, tie and trim the thread off

Shirts

Method 1 – Weave Darning

1. Use a darning mushroom or darning egg to stretch the fabric

2. Thread your needle with a matching color and sew back and forth over the hole. Ensure the stitches are long enough to cover the hole. It's worth noting that you should not knot your thread.

N.B: This weave darning method is a little different and simpler than the method illustrated in chapter 4, under *Darning Techniques – Weave Darning.* So you can choose to use the method below or that described in chapter 4; the choice is yours. Remember, clothe mending is not caste-in-stone; hence there is room for creativity and ingenuity.

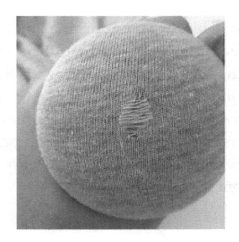

3. When you've finished stitching in one way, you can flip your fabric at 90 degrees and begin to sew back and forth. This time, go beneath and across the individual stitch to weave between the stitches you've previously made

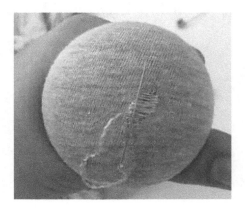

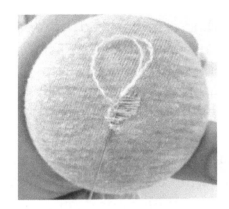

4. Once the entire area has been covered, secure the thread with a few stitches in your weave without knots!

5. You should have something like the one below when you are done

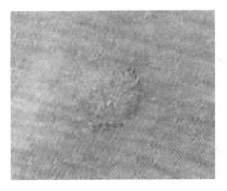

The weave darn can be used to repair any fabric, just ensure you use a thread that is the same color and thickness as the fabric being repaired.

Method 2 – Embroidery

The embroidery design used to mend the hole in the shirt below is the eye-shaped "leaf" design. Remember you can use any pattern or design you feel comfortable with to cover up your hole. As I mentioned earlier, these free embroidery patterns are freely accessible over the internet. So, do not limit yourself to a particular design.

1. First, cut off any rough edges and loose ends of yarn around the hole area.

2. Make an eye-shaped "leaf" design using a chalk pencil or any other vanishing marker around the hole, then place an embroidery hoop around the hole area to give your garment a good tension to work with.

3. Measure a long length of embroidery thread that will be sufficient to embroider the leaf design, fold the thread in half and tie a knot at the end.

4. Following the pattern design you made (apologies, you'd be unable to clearly see the design pattern made in the image below; however, yours should be visible to stitch), push up the needle on your leaf's tip via the underneath side of the fabric.

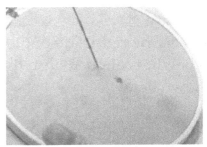

5. Return the stitching to the center (close to the hole) as shown below, bringing it up to the left side.

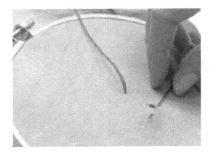

6. Enter through the leaf's top right tip and exit through the top left.

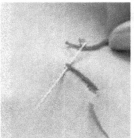

7. Move down to the right side of the center and ensure its height is aligned with that of the right side, as shown below.

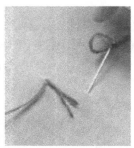

8. Pull out the needle on the left just beneath the preceding stitch.

9. Continue in the same sequence until you get to the end and the hole area is covered up.

Socks

Method 1 – Swiss Darning or Duplicate Stitch

The swiss darning or duplicate stitch method is most suitable for holes that are so small or worn areas that are on the verge of becoming a hole.

1. We'll start our duplicate stitch roughly 1" distant from the spot we want to reinforce/ repair by using a darning or tapestry needle with a thread that's about 10-12." Insert your needle beneath the right-hand side of one of your stitch's "V's."

Pull it back up via the center of the "V."

2. This "V" will be duplicated above the "knit" in which the thread just appeared through the center. To do this, push your needle beneath both legs of the "V," i.e., the two legs on top where we came in from. Pull the end of the thread, making it a little tight.

3. Now you'll enter the center of that initial "V," coming back up the center of the "V" to the left of that stitch.

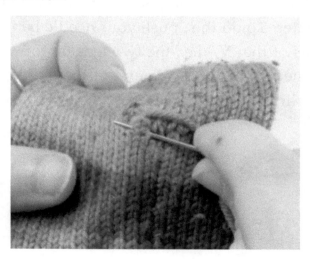

4. Repeat steps 2–3 all the way around the weak portion of your sock. If you have to stitch over numerous rows, skip to the subsequent row of V's by simply going up to a higher "V" upon completing a row. You may have a tough time matching the tension of your stitching with that of the torn/ worn out spot; so if this is the case, insert a darning mushroom or egg inside the sock.

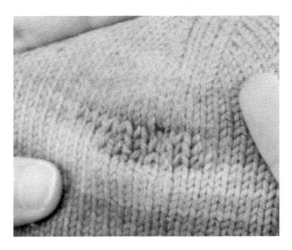

If you sew with the original color of the socks, you will have invisible darning, as you can see. Spotting holes in your socks early on before they appear and reinforcing them will minimize their visibility, especially if you don't appreciate a visible darn.

Method 2 – Woven Patch

Darning socks using the woven patch method, which is the same as "weave darning," is arguably the most well-known method. You can use this method to repair bigger holes in your sock, unlike the swiss darning method. One drawback of the woven patch method is that it uses the weaving technique, unlike the swiss darning, which uses the knitting technique; thus, you will end up with a visible repair. For this reason, using a complementary but contrasting thread to weave your patches might help a little.

Weaving is not as elastic as knitting; therefore, you need to use a darning egg for this method else your socks will end up not fitting properly if you weave your patch without it.

1. Thread your needle, using your preferred thread in weaving the patch and sew a basting (running stitch) stitch around the hole to form a square. This will help in securing the patch while also reinforcing any stitches that haven't yet worn out.

2. Make a warp for the patch by tucking the thread underneath the legs of stitches and running it across the square.

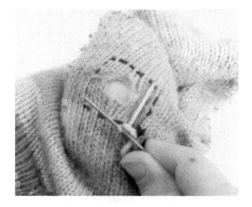

3. This should be done all the way across the basted square.

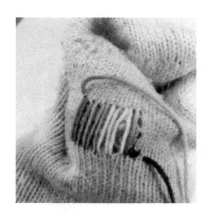

4. Perpendicularly weave your weft to your warp. This is done when you go across and beneath each warp thread. In between every weft pass, ensure to tack down the weft by going in/out of a stitch. This will hold the woven patch in place and prevent your weaving from becoming too tight.

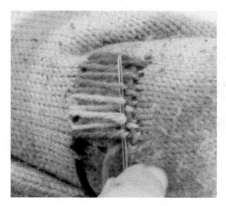

5. When you've run out of warp to weave beneath, simply weave in your ends as you deem fit, and you're finished!

6. A sock that has been successfully mended!

You can see how much the woven section shrinks once you remove the darning egg, so a darning egg should always be used when you use the weave darning method.

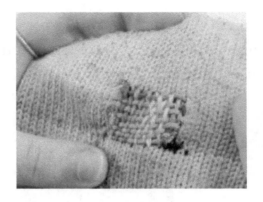

You will also notice that this weave darning method used here is more in tune with the *Darning Techniques – Weave Darning* in chapter 4, unlike the simpler method adopted under the repair of "**Shirts**" in the previous section.

Sweaters

Weave Darning Method

The weave darning method described below for this sweater is similar to the process I described in the woven patch method above, except that the semantics of the illustration is different from each other. So, don't be confused.

1. Insert a darning mushroom or egg beneath the hole to provide a good work surface.

2. Pick a good place to start sewing; ideally, a distance of about 1cm or so, beneath and to the side of the hole. Thread your darning or tapestry needle and push up the needle from behind to the front, as shown below. Leave some inches of tail (without knots) to enable you to weave into the back after you're done with the whole mending process.

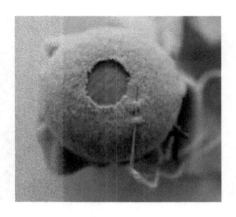

3. The warp, the "weave" that goes up and down, is the first thing we need to sew. From where you started, sew a running stitch that is parallel to and within the original fabric's weave while continuing upwards to a spot above the hole, with small dashes of thread - the distance should be identical to where you began your first stitch, i.e., beneath the hole. As soon as you've gotten to the desired distance, flip the direction of your sewing and continue stitching, just next and parallel to the previous stitch.

Continue stitching up and down, but ensure to position the stitches (or "seed stitches") in a random pattern so they don't end up next to each other.

4. On getting to the hole, make a long stitch that crosses over the hole and continue to sew on the other side. Ensure the stitches you make across the hole are close together because this is where the major repair will be done, and you'll want it (the woven section) to be thick. Bear in mind also that you can vary the distance of your stitching into the original fabric. You may decide that the seed stitches create a clean border for the repair, or you can leave them with an uneven and organic look like I did here.

5. It is okay to switch your thread color at this point if you so desire to add some variation. I choose to vary the color, though little, so that the warp isn't all one color. This can create some visual interest to the mend while also giving it a more personalized appearance. Simply leave a tail underneath the original fabric and stop stitching somewhere within the previous stitch.

Start the new color with a tail underneath it, as you did at the beginning of the mending process, and continue to create the warp. Once completed, these tails will be weaved onto the back. Upon covering the hole, continue stitching into the fabric to a distance comparable to how you started to ensure the mend is anchored evenly on all sides.

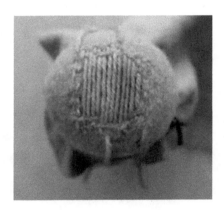

6. The weft, or the stitches running from side to side, weaving into the warp, is the next phase. For this phase, I used a third color.

   Basically, start beneath and to one side of the hole, as you did with the warp, and continue stitching in the same way by first anchoring seed stitches back and forth within the original fabric. I wasn't concerned with my spacing in this case because I wanted the stitches to be a bit random, but on getting to where the hole will be bridged or connected with longer stitches, you'll have to weave the weft's thread into the warp's thread. This is done when you slide the needle beneath and over the warp threads and pull the needle thread through.

7. To continue weaving subsequent rows of stitches in the reverse direction, ensure you weave in the reverse direction to the stitch of the previous row; for example, if the previous thread line was beneath / above, the subsequent thread line will be above/ beneath. This ensures the repair made on the hole is more secure and durable.

Now, continue stitching back and forth as you previously did until you have weaved and covered the hole and with each stitch anchored into the original fabric at the sides.

Upon completion, tidy up by pulling loose thread tails on your needle to the back if they aren't already there and rethreading them. Then, make a running stitch right into the weave on the back to secure them; cut the loose tails.

Conclusion

Phew!

This brings us to the end of a wonderful read. If you read through each page of this book to the end, then I say congratulations; you epitomize the traits of someone that is willing to succeed.

In the pages of this book, we discussed to a great extent, most of the information you need to start mending your clothes today while also becoming your own hero in contributing to a sustainable culture of "reducing, reusing, and recycling." All you need to get started are a needle, thread, and a few basic stitching skills. It is a skill anyone can learn with the right mental attitude to the idea of repairing worn-out clothes instead of trashing them in the bin, plus the willingness and consistency required to master the craft of mending clothes.

While learning to use your clothes for long durations serves to benefit the environment around you, you would also be drawn to the personal benefits of mending regularly. It is empowering to learn a new skill, particularly one that allows us to become increasingly self-sufficient and less dependent on destructive systems. Mending provides us the peace of mind of understanding that when a garment shows symptoms of deterioration, we won't have to waste time looking for something and then spending money on it. With mending, we have most of what we need in our homes and heads to get by.

Furthermore, mending is a mindfulness exercise. It's relaxing, meditative, and sensual to stitch and mend clothes. It forces you to cherish your clothes more deeply by bringing you closer to the things on which you depend. Mending the clothes that we love and that we feel good about improves the perception we have of ourselves, which in turn changes the world around us for the better.

Printed in the USA
CPSIA information can be obtained
at www.ICGtesting.com
LVHW010319030924
789951LV00030B/1164